# Inspiring Civil Rights Movement Stories for Children

*True Tales of Courage, Equality, and Change to Bring History to Life for Children*

# Welcome Aboard, Check Out This Limited-Time Free Bonus!

Ahoy, reader! Welcome to the Ahoy Publications family, and thanks for snagging a copy of this book! Since you've chosen to join us on this journey, we'd like to offer you something special.

Check out the link below for a FREE e-book filled with delightful facts about American History.

But that's not all - you'll also have access to our exclusive email list with even more free e-books and insider knowledge. Well, what are ye waiting for? Click the link below to join and set sail toward exciting adventures in American History.

Access your bonus here

https://ahoypublications.com/

Or, Scan the QR code!

# Table of Contents

# Introduction

Imagine living in a world where the color of your skin decides where you could live. Your skin color might determine what school you went to, where you could eat, and if you could play at a park. It even decided if your parents could vote. These were the struggles African Americans faced before the Civil Rights Movement.

This book shares real stories from that time. You'll read about kids who faced angry crowds just to go to school. You'll learn about students who protested because they were not served food. You'll meet heroes who held peaceful demonstrations to fight for change. Their actions changed the world and showed that courage has no age.

As you read, you'll meet heroes, young and old. You'll see how boycotts, sit-ins, court cases, and protests helped end unfair laws. Think about what you would do in their place.

During the Civil Rights Movement, people your age stood up for freedom and fairness. Their stories prove that bravery comes in all shapes and sizes. Anyone, no matter their age, can help make the world better.

As you turn the pages, imagine yourself living in that time. How would you feel? What would you do? And how can their courage inspire you to make a difference today?

# Chapter One: Rosa Parks and the Montgomery Bus Boycott

Imagine going back to 1955 in Montgomery, Alabama. Life was very different then. There were no cell phones or computers. Video games didn't exist. Color TVs were new, but most people couldn't afford them.

Life in the 1950s was harder for African Americans. Slavery ended in 1865 with the 13th Amendment. But Black people were still not treated fairly, especially in the South.

Montgomery was called the birthplace of the Civil Rights Movement. In 1955, the city had about 106,000 people. Almost 40 percent were Black. But Black people didn't have the same rights as White people. Their daily lives were much harder.

Segregation was a big part of life, then. Blacks were not allowed to shop in certain stores. They could check out books only from Black libraries. If they wanted a drink of water, they had to make sure they drank from the right fountain.

The same went for parks and other places of relaxation. Only certain areas were available for them. Kids attended different schools, which usually had supplies and buildings of inferior quality. Not everyone could afford a vehicle. Public transportation was important for getting to work, school, and running errands.

However, Black people had specific seats where they had to sit. If the seats were full, they'd have to give theirs up if a White passenger wanted it.

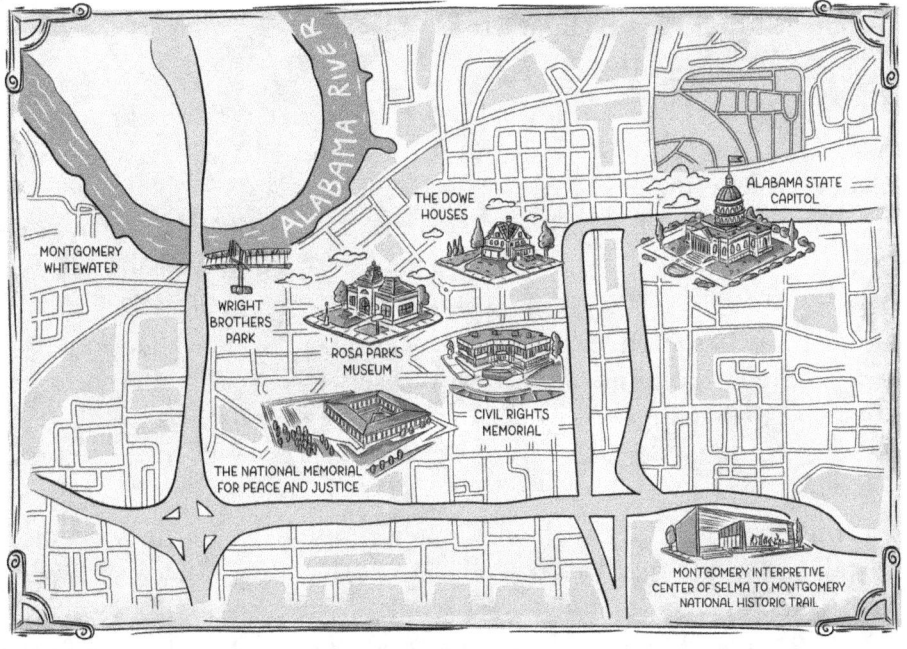

Rosa Parks was a Black woman who worked as a seamstress in a department store. She took the bus to work every day. By the end of her shift, she was exhausted. Of course, her feet hurt. December 1, 1955, was a cold day in Montgomery, Alabama. Rosa boarded the bus, as she always did after work. She knew the bus rules; Blacks had to sit in the back section. She walked to the fifth row, which was the first row of the "colored section," and sat in a window seat (U.S. History).

The bus filled up, though. The bus driver, James Blake, told Rosa and three other Black people to move to other seats so White passengers could sit closer to the front of the vehicle. The others moved, but Rosa refused to give her seat to the White man waiting. U.S. History recalled the conversation that followed.

*"Are you going to stand up?" Asked Blake, the driver.*

*Rosa looked at him and said: "No."*

*Flustered, Blake warned: "Well, I'm going to have you arrested."*

*Rosa continued to sit in her seat by the window and softly said: "You may do that."*

He did. The authorities came and arrested Rosa. She spent only a few hours in jail. She was bailed out by civil rights leader Edgar Nixon and Attorney Clifford and his wife Virginia Durr – who were both White (Library of Congress). Rosa lost her case in court and was fined $14, which today would equal about $165.

### The Montgomery Bus Boycott

At this time, Martin Luther King Jr. was not yet well known. He would later go on to become one of the nation's leading civil rights activists. He became very famous for his "I Have a Dream" speech. He and Ralph Abernathy belonged to the Montgomery Improvement Association. They got together and organized a boycott of the buses in the city after Rosa's arrest (U.S. History).

The boycott started just four days later, on Monday, December 5. The Women's Political Council advertised it with a leaflet. It asked people not to take buses to work, town, school, or *anywhere* on Monday. Instead, people could take a cab, share a ride, or walk to their work." (U.S. History).

Word got out, and it worked. People refused to ride the city buses. Instead, they rode in Black-owned cabs or in their own cars together. Some even walked as much as 20 miles to get to their destinations (NAACP). The bus company lost a lot of money. Officials tried everything they could to stop the protest. Violence broke out in the city. Martin Luther King Jr. and Ralph Abernathy were arrested, and their homes were bombed, as were four churches (U.S. History).

Finally, nearly a year later, on November 23, 1957, the boycott ended after the Supreme Court ruling Browder v. Gayle found that it was unconstitutional to have segregation on buses.

Rosa Parks had already left town by this time. After her arrest, she lost her job. Her husband quit his job because he wasn't allowed to speak about his wife's case. The couple moved away from Montgomery in 1957 (Biography).

The Montgomery Bus Boycott started because Rosa Parks stood up to unfair segregation laws. Her courage inspired more protests and the fight for civil rights.

In 1964, Congress passed the Civil Rights Act. This law banned segregation in public places and jobs. By the late 1960s, segregation ended in Alabama (Encyclopedia).

Rosa continued fighting for civil rights throughout the rest of her long life. In her autobiography, *Rosa Parks: My Story* (1992), she said what she did that day on the bus, refusing to give up her seat to a White man, was intentional. Rosa Parks said she wasn't tired in her body, even after working hard all day. She wasn't old – she was only 42 years old. But Rosa was very tired of giving in to unfair rules. (NAACP).

**Activity**

Imagine you are Rosa Parks that day on the bus. Write a diary entry explaining the day's events.

**Quiz**

1. Martin Luther King Jr. was already a well-known activist when he helped start the Montgomery Bus Boycott. (T/F)
2. Montgomery, Alabama, is known as the birthplace of the Civil Rights Movement. (T/F)
3. After the boycott ended, Rosa and her husband stayed in Montgomery to continue fighting for Civil Rights (T/F)
4. Congress passed the Civil Rights Act, ending segregation a year after the bus boycott. (T/F)
5. Some people walked 20 miles during the boycott. (T/F)

**Answers**

1. F
2. T
3. F
4. F
5. T

# Chapter Two: The Courage of the Little Rock Nine

In the 1950s, life was very hard for African Americans, especially in the South. Even their children couldn't go to the same school as White children. It was unfair, but in 1954, something very important happened in America. The Supreme Court said it was against the law to keep Black and White children in separate schools. It made this decision and the case was called *Brown v. The Board of Education.*

It was only two years after Rosa Parks had refused to give up her bus seat. In 1957, nine Black students started going to an all-White school in Little Rock, Arkansas. They were very brave because it was so hard for Black children to go to White schools then. Others bullied them and said mean things. Some even tried to hurt them. But these brave students, called the "Little Rock Nine," stayed strong as rocks and kept going.

Elizabeth Eckford. [1]

Virgil Blossom, the school superintendent, had an idea. He wanted Black and White students to go to the same school. He would start it with his school. The school board asked for volunteers from two Black schools. How many signed up? Nine students, Minnijean Brown, Gloria Ray, Elizabeth Eckford, Melba Pattillo, Terrence Roberts, Thelma Mothershed, Jefferson Thomas, Ernest Green, and Carlotta Walls, wanted to join.

Minnijean Brown said, "When my teacher said we might go to a White school, I signed up. Central High School had more courses, a stadium, and tennis courts (National Park Service)."

But Carlotta Walls remembered the things they could not do in the new school. She said, "They told us we couldn't go to sports games, the prom, or join school clubs. There were so many things we couldn't do (National Park Service)."

Elizabeth Eckford said, "I wasn't ready for what happened (National Park Service)."

The governor, Orval Faubus, sent soldiers from the National Guard to the school the night before the school was going to start.

It was to keep the peace, he said, but the soldiers wouldn't let the Black students get in (National Park Service).

Thelma Mothershed said, "I thought they [the guards] were there to protect me. I was wrong."

Jefferson Thomas said, "We didn't know keeping peace was to keep us out."

The Black students saw groups of angry people outside the school on the first day. Both the soldiers and the people didn't want Black children to enter the school.

Only Elizabeth Eckford came to school.

People shouted, "Two, four, six, eight." They rhymed and teased and didn't want their kids to mix with Black children (National Park Service).

Two weeks later, on September 23, the nine students tried to go to school again. But riots broke out, and the police had to take the students away to keep them safe. The situation was very dangerous.

President Dwight D. Eisenhower decided to help. On September 24, 1957, he took control of the state's National Guard. Now, the National Guard had to follow the President's orders. President Eisenhower also sent soldiers from the Army's 101st Airborne Division, called the "Screaming Eagles," to Little Rock (National Park Service). He said, "We cannot let mobs stop the Court's decisions."

Finally, on September 25, the nine students entered the school building. This happened after 18 days of protests by people who didn't want change. But going to school was still very hard for them. Each student had a guard to walk them to their classes.

Things didn't get easier for the Little Rock Nine once they started going to school. Each student had a guard to walk them to class, but the guards couldn't go everywhere. They weren't allowed in classrooms, bathrooms, or locker rooms. This meant that Black students were bullied and called mean names when no one was watching.

The 101st Airborne Division soldiers escorted African-American students to Central High School in Little Rock in Sept. 1957.'

Minnijean Brown had a hard time. She accidentally spilled chili on some boys who wouldn't let her sit in the cafeteria. Later, she called a girl a mean name after the girl hit her with a purse. Because of this, Minnijean was expelled from school. After she left, some students passed cards that said, "One Down, Eight to Go." (National Park Service).

At the end of the year, the city closed its high schools to stop Black and White students from learning together. The NAACP fought in court to reopen the schools. When the schools reopened, Carlotta Walls and Jefferson Thomas returned. Both graduated in 1960.

Ernest Green was already a senior when he joined Central High. In 1958, he became the first Black person to graduate from the school. "It's been an interesting year," Ernest told a magazine. "I've learned a lot about people."

### What became of the Little Rock Nine?

When they grew up, the Little Rock Nine did many great things.

Minnijean Brown went to college and got two degrees. She helped people and worked with President Bill Clinton. Elizabeth Eckford studied history and joined the Army. Ernest Green went to college and worked with Presidents Bill Clinton and Jimmy Carter. Thelma Mothershed became a teacher and helped kids in school. Melba Pattillo went to school and worked on TV and radio. Gloria Ray studied science and math. She helped make robots.

Terrence Roberts learned about how people think and started his own business. Jefferson Thomas joined the Army. Carlotta Walls went to college and learned about land and buildings. She started her own business. They all worked hard and made the world a better place!

## Activity

Create a poster or drawing that represents courage in the face of adversity.

## Multiple Choice Quiz

1. Little Rock is a city in which state?

    A. Alabama

    B. Arkansas

    C. Arizona

2. Which Supreme Court case said schools shouldn't separate between Black and White students?

    A. Brown v. The Board of Education

    B. Little Rock v. The Board of Education

    C. Black v. The Board of Education

3. Which President sent the National Guard to protect the Little Rock Nine?

    A. Thomas Jefferson

    B. Dwight D. Eisenhower

    C. Jimmy Carter

4. What was the superintendent's name who wanted Black students to attend White schools?

    A. Johnathon Gibbs

    B. Dwight Mayors

    C. Virgil Blossom

5. In what year did the Little Rock Nine start classes at Central High School?

    A. 1957

    B. 1956

    C. 1955

**Answers**

1. B
2. A
3. B
4. C
5. A

# Chapter Three: Martin Luther King Jr. and the March to Washington

In the 1960s, life was different for Black and White people.

The economy was growing. White workers earned more money. But African Americans made much less. Black and White people were separated in schools, jobs, and public places.

### Martin Luther King Jr.

A Black preacher, Martin Luther King Jr. was also a leader for justice and loved the idea of peace. He was driven by the need to see a better world. King Jr. believed everyone should be treated equally, no matter their skin color.

He worked hard to bring change through peaceful protests. Even in the hardest times, he believed peace, not fighting, was the answer to a better world.

King's father, Martin Luther King Sr., was also a preacher. He taught his children to understand racism was wrong and against God's will. King Jr. looked up to his father and learned from his strong beliefs.

In college, King became passionate about politics and fairness. He wanted to help African Americans gain the same rights as everyone else. He once said, "I could see myself helping to break the legal barriers."

King was a leader in many civil rights events. He helped with the Montgomery Bus Boycott after Rosa Parks protested against segregation. He did a lot for people at the time, but most of all, he gave them hope. He gave many speeches to inspire people, including the famous "I Have a Dream" speech, where he shared his vision of a world where everyone is treated equally.

He said six things lead to peace. Let's take a look at what they are:

- Be brave.
- Make friends and try to understand others.
- Fight unfair laws, not people.
- Suffering for a good cause can teach others.
- Choose love, not hate.
- Believe that justice will win.

## March on Washington

March on Washington.[a]

Nearly ten years after Rosa Parks was told to give up her seat to a White man, things for Blacks had not improved much. There were still many without jobs; those who did work were paid low wages, and racial segregation was still going on. So, King and others decided to march in the nation's capital to bring attention to the problem.

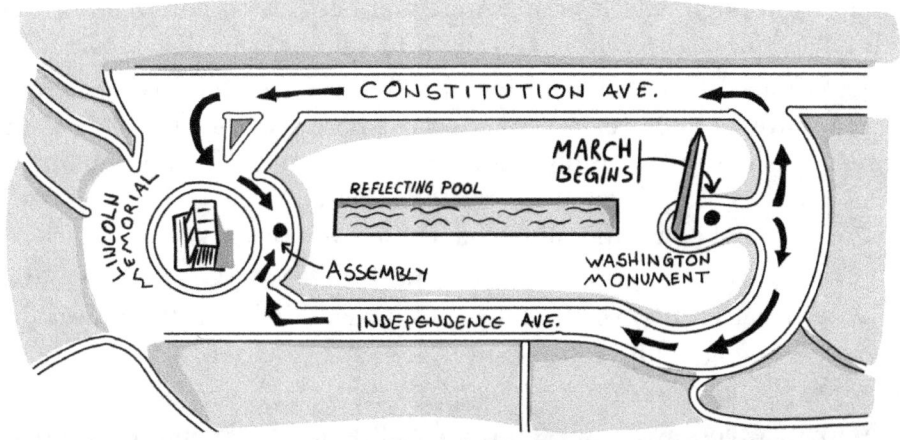

Martin Luther King Jr. '

More than 250,000 people gathered near the Lincoln Memorial and the Reflecting Pool in Washington, D.C., on a sunny day in 1963. They were of all ages and colors, and they came from all over the country. Some had walked for miles to be there. They came with hope and dreams for a better future.

Dr. Martin Luther King Jr. stepped up to the microphone. The crowd became quiet, ready to listen. He looked at all the people and began his famous speech, "I Have a Dream." Dr. King talked about the hard times Black people faced. He reminded everyone that even though slavery had ended, Black people were still not treated fairly. They lived with unfair rules, segregation, and discrimination.

Dr. King's words were sad but also full of hope. He told the crowd about his dream. He dreamed of a world where everyone was treated the same, no matter the color of their skin. He dreamed of a time when kids of all races could play together. He dreamed of a day when Black Americans would have the same chances as everyone else.

Dr. King's march on Washington and his speech showed how unfair life was for Black people. If you could imagine being in the crowd that day and listening to Dr. King's powerful words, you, too, would feel how everyone else felt: *hope and strength.*

Many people saw his speech on TV. It made a big difference; many came forward and wanted to help. More and more people joined the Civil Rights Movement. All over the country, people marched, protested, and spoke out against unfair rules.

Just one year later, a new law was made in 1964. The Civil Rights Act stopped the separation or segregation of Black and White people in public places. People could no longer treat each other unfairly because of their race.

Dr. King was one of the greatest leaders of the Civil Rights Movement. His dreams and words helped with other events held against segregation. Some of these were the Montgomery Bus Boycott and marches in Alabama. It led to the creation of important new laws, like the Voting Rights Act of 1965.

In 1964, at just 35 years old, Dr. King won the Nobel Peace Prize for his efforts. Dr. King's words showed how strong everyone could be when they stood together peacefully. It gave them hope and courage. His dreams still inspire us today. They tell everyone to treat others with kindness and to stand up for what is right.

## Quiz

1. Martin Luther King Jr.'s famous speech was called:

   A) I Have a Dream

   B) I Have a Wish

   C) I Have Hope

2. Martin Luther King Jr. was a _____ who worked hard for civil rights.

   A) Catholic priest

   B) Protestant minister

   C) Baptist minister

3. Martin Jr. had six rules of _____.

   A) Nonviolence

   B) Avoiding racism

   C) Delivering speeches

4. One of Dr. King's six rules of nonviolence says that nonviolence means believing that the world is on the side of _____.

   A) The law

   B) Racism

   C) Justice

5. The March on Washington was about _____.

   A) Segregation on buses

   B) Jobs and freedom

   C) Fulfilling dreams

## Activity

Close your eyes and imagine a better world. What do you wish for? Do you dream of kids being friends no matter who they are? Write down "I have a dream" at the top of the page. Then, write a few sentences about your dream. Use crayons or markers to draw what your dream looks like. Now, your speech is ready! Read it out to your family or friends.

## Answers

1. A
2. C
3. A
4. C
5. B

# Chapter Four: The Freedom Riders: Journeys for Justice

Who was the famous Black woman who refused to give up her seat on a bus? Yes, it was Rosa Parks. But she wasn't the first. Much before her, Irene Morgan said no when told to move for a White passenger. This was in 1944. Irene was arrested, but she fought back. The NAACP supported her case, and in 1956, the Supreme Court ruled that segregation on interstate buses was illegal (PBS).

Even though the court said segregation was wrong, it still happened in the South. Black people were forced to sit in the back of buses. On trains, they had to ride in separate cars. They couldn't use the same restrooms, lunch counters, or waiting areas as White people. Many people were tired of these unfair rules. To show how wrong it was, the Congress of Racial Equality (CORE) organized Freedom Rides. Black and White riders rode together through the South. It was to show that segregation, although illegal, was still happening.

These rides were peaceful, but the riders still faced angry mobs, arrests, and violence. They were brave and didn't give up. Their courage to face these problems helped show everyone how deeply rooted segregation was. It inspired others to join the fight for civil rights.

## The Freedom Riders

Students protesting against the segregation of Black and White people formed the Congress of Racial Equality (CORE) in 1961. On May 4, CORE began the Freedom Rides through the South. The ride was dangerous, and sometimes there was violence.

Freedom Rider Charles Person remembered how dangerous the ride was. "You could be attacked at any time. Planning a trip was very hard," he said (PBS).

There were seven Black riders and six White riders in the first group. They left Washington, D.C., to travel to New Orleans, Louisiana. The trouble began on May 12 in Rock Hill, South Carolina. Some people attacked riders who tried to use a Whites-only waiting area (History).

### The Burning of a Freedom Riders Bus

Freedom Riders bus. ⁵

On May 14, 1961, a Greyhound bus stopped in Anniston, Alabama. An angry group of about 200 White people surrounded the bus. The driver was scared and didn't stop but drove past the station. The angry group got into cars and chased the bus. When the tires went flat, the driver had to stop. The mob came closer and threw a bomb at the bus. The Freedom Riders got out, but the mob attacked them and hurt them badly.

Pictures of the burning bus and hurt people were in newspapers everywhere. Another bus of Freedom Riders was attacked in Birmingham, Alabama. Bull Conner, the man in charge of keeping the city safe, didn't send the police to help. He said it was because it was Mother's Day.

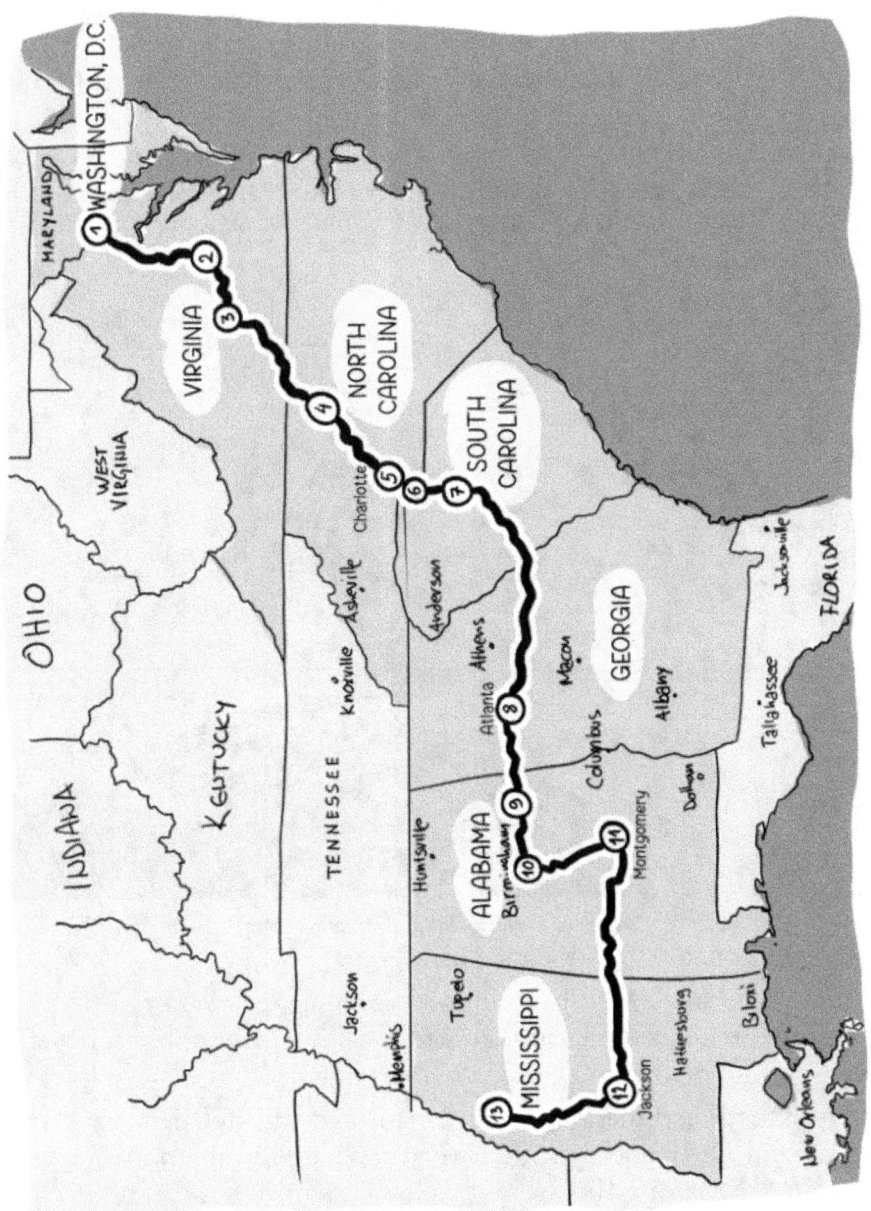

It was hard to find bus drivers for the Freedom Riders because of the violence. CORE, the group running the rides, had to stop. But a new group, SNCC, decided to help. Diane Nash, a leader in SNCC, asked ten students from Nashville to keep the rides going (History).

Even though they were attacked again, the Freedom Riders didn't give up. A government leader, Robert F. Kennedy, tried to help. To find people to drive, he talked to the governor of Alabama. The rides began again on May 20. Police were following a bus that left Birmingham to make sure it was safe. The cops left, though, before the bus got to Montgomery. A group of people with bats and sticks struck the riders. Robert F. Kennedy sent 600 federal agents to protect the Freedom Riders (History).

Segregated bathrooms and drinking water. °

People still treated the Freedom Riders badly and put them in danger. On May 24, 1961, things seemed to get better. In Jackson, Mississippi, many people came to support them. But police arrested the Freedom Riders when they used "Whites only" places.

The Freedom Riders stayed peaceful and did not fight back. News stations and newspapers showed what happened to them. More people joined the Freedom Riders and helped them. The Freedom Riders' bravery caused big changes. By November 1, 1961, buses had stopped separating Black and White people. Workers took down the "Whites only" signs.

## Quiz

Can you say which of these statements are true (T) and which are false (F)?

1. Irene Morgan was arrested for not giving up her seat on a bus to a White person a decade earlier than Rosa Parks.
   - T
   - F

2. The Freedom Riders were made up of Black students fighting against segregation.
   - T
   - F

3. President Ronald Reagan was in office when the Freedom Riders demonstration was happening.
   - T
   - F

4. The burning of a bus happened in Mississippi.
   - T
   - F

5. In Alabama, the public safety commissioner, Bull Conner, knew there would be violence but didn't send out police protection because it was Mother's Day.
   - T
   - F

## Activity

Pretend to be a Freedom Rider, and think about how they felt and what they wanted to change. Make your own Freedom Rider notes in your diary! Are you feeling brave, scared, or hopeful? Did you try to sit in a "Whites-only" area? Why do you think it's important to do this? Write about your hopes here.

**Answers:**

1. T
2. F (White people too)
3. F
4. F
5. T

# Chapter Five: Ruby Bridges: A Young Girl Makes History

Families struggled because most jobs didn't pay much money. The law said segregation was unfair. Still, the government used tricky words to keep Black families separated from White families. One was "urban renewal," which meant the work of cleaning and repairing the cities (Gray, D. Ryan). Black children were not allowed to go to school with White children and had separate schools. This hurt people. Things started to change because of a six-year-old girl. Her name was Ruby Bridges. She was the first Black child who went to an all-White school in New Orleans.

### Ruby Bridges

Ruby Bridges was born in 1954. That was the same year the Supreme Court ruled in *Brown v. Board of Education* that separating schools by race was unfair. The court said schools had to desegregate. But in Louisiana, it took six more years before this started.

In 1960, Ruby became the first Black child to attend an all-White school. It was a big step, but it wasn't easy.

Ruby was chosen because she was one of six Black children who passed a special test. This test allowed her to go to a White school. Her parents wanted her to get a better education. Neither of them had finished school.

Ruby's mother left school in eighth grade to help her family. She wanted Ruby to have more chances. Ruby's father was worried. He thought it would be dangerous. Many White people didn't want Black children in their schools. But Ruby's mother convinced him. She believed Ruby could help make things better (Dawson, Shay).

## Ruby's First Year at School

U.S. Marshals escort Ruby Bridges. '

U.S. Marshals had to walk with Ruby Bridges to keep her safe. Parents were angry that she was allowed to go to school with their kids. They stood outside and protested.

On her first day, Ruby stayed in the principal's office. It was too dangerous for her to join the other students. Many White parents took their kids out of school because Ruby was there. In the end, Ruby was the only student in her class. Her teacher, Barbara Henry, was a White woman from Boston. She taught Ruby alone for her whole first-grade year (Dawson, Shay).

Every day, Ruby went to school with her mom and the marshals. She sat in the classroom with just her teacher. She wasn't allowed to talk to the White students. Ruby brought her own lunch from home because people worried someone might poison her food (Dawson, Shay).

Ruby didn't play outside during recess. She stayed inside and played games with her teacher. Even when she needed to use the bathroom, the marshals walked her there to keep her safe. Ruby had to deal with a lot, but she was brave and went to school every day.

Ruby Bridges wasn't the only one who had a hard time going to an all-White school. Her parents lost their jobs because of what she did. They had to get help from others to take care of the family. Even Ruby's grandparents, who lived in Mississippi, were affected by the anger of people (Dawson, Shay).

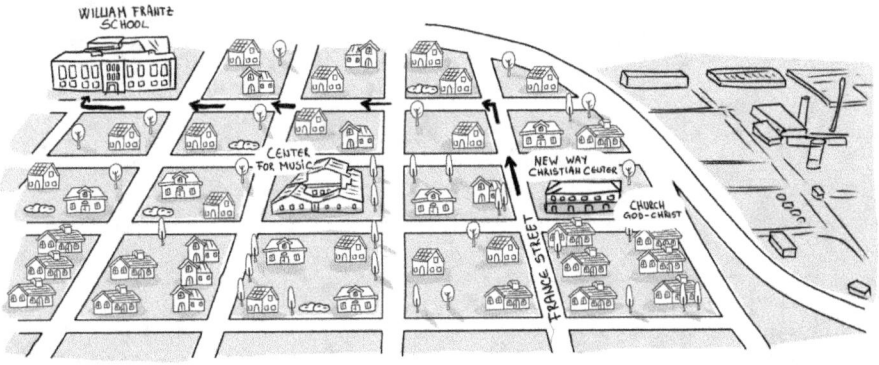

By Ruby's second year at school, some things changed. More White people started to accept her. She was no longer the only Black student at the school.

Ruby's bravery inspired many people. One of them was Norman Rockwell, a famous artist. In 1963, he painted *The Problem We All*

*Live With.* The painting shows Ruby walking into school with U.S. Marshals protecting her. The artwork got mixed reactions, but it showed the whole country how brave Ruby was at just six years old (Dawson, Shay).

Ruby grew up and continued to fight for civil rights. In 2000, she was named an honorary Deputy U.S. Marshal. In 2010, she was honored at the White House. She entered into the National Women's Hall of Fame in 2024 (Dawson, Shay).

## Quiz: Two Truths and a Lie

In this quiz, you are given two truths and a lie – can you spot the lie?

**1.**

A) Ruby Bridges was six years old when she attended the all-White school.

B) Ruby Bridges went to an all-White school located in Mississippi.

C) Ruby Bridges' parents never finished school.

**2.**

A) Ruby received an honor at the White House.

B) Ruby entered into the National Women's Hall of Fame.

C) Ruby received the Nobel Peace Prize.

**3.**

A) Ruby ate lunch in the cafeteria.

B) U.S. Marshals had to escort Ruby to the bathroom.

C) Ruby was the only student in her classroom.

## Activity

Write a thank-you letter to Ruby Bridges. You don't have to write a lot. Write from your heart and imagine how Ruby might feel reading your letter! You can write about how hard it must have been for her to go to school when people were so mean. Say how she made a difference and how her actions helped other kids. You can end with something nice, like how her story inspired you to be kind to others.

**Answers**

1. B
2. C
3. A

# Chapter Six: The Greensboro Sit-In

In the 1960s, Black and White people were still kept apart. Black people couldn't use the same bathrooms, go to the same schools, or drink from the same water fountains as White people. They also couldn't eat at lunch counters in some stores and restaurants. Four brave students in Greensboro, North Carolina, wanted to change this. They started a protest called the Greensboro Sit-In.

## The Greensboro Sit-In

Greensboro Sit-In at Woolworth's counter. [9]

Four Black men named Franklin McCain, Joseph McNeil, Ezell Blair Jr., and David Richmond were called the Greensboro Four (History). They were students at a school in North Carolina. On February 1, 1960, they went to Woolworth's lunch counter, where Black people were not allowed. The four men sat down and asked for food, even though they knew the store wouldn't serve them.

The men were told they couldn't be served and were asked to leave. But they stayed in their seats and didn't give up. They were polite and calm, even when the police came. Since the men weren't doing anything wrong, the police couldn't arrest them. The students had planned their protest before they went. A White businessman named Ralph Johns helped them. Johns told reporters what was happening, and TV cameras came to film it. The four students remained in their seats until the store shut down.

The next day, the four students came back to the store. This time, more students came with them. In a few days, 300 students were sitting in the store. The store had a problem. They couldn't serve other customers because so many people were sitting. The group said everyone should sit together as equals (National Museum of American History).

People saw the sit-ins on TV. The news spread to other towns. Soon, students in other places started sit-ins. They sat in libraries, hotels, and on beaches (History).

### The Impact of Greensboro Sit-In

By the summer of 1960, some restaurants began to change their rules. They started serving Black people. The Greensboro Woolworth's changed its rule, too. Four Black employees – Charles Best, Anetha Jones, Susie Morrison, and Geneva Tisdale – were the first to eat there (History).

Two months after the sit-ins started, a group called SNCC was formed in Raleigh, North Carolina. This group helped organize the Freedom Rides in 1961 and the March on Washington in 1963. That was when Dr. King gave his famous "I Have a Dream" speech.

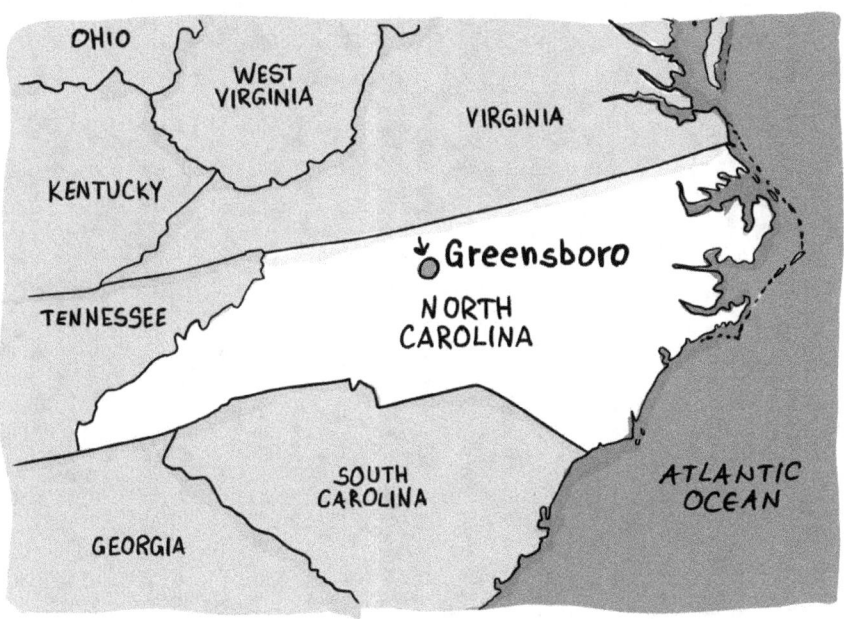

It showed peaceful protests can make a difference. The sit-ins helped get more rights for Black people. The Civil Rights Act came because of these protests. A museum in Washington, D.C., still has a section of this lunch counter. The Woolworth's building in Greensboro is now a Civil Rights Museum (History).

The Greensboro Sit-In was very important for Black people in American history (History). It helped share the fight for fairness across the country. This was called the civil rights movement. Civil meant people.

People protested peacefully and inspired others to fight for fair treatment. These protests helped make a law called the Civil Rights Act.

Everyone must obey the law. Black people could now receive fair treatment.

What happened to the lunch counter at Woolworth's where it all started? Part of it is in a museum in Washington, D.C. The old Woolworth's store in Greensboro is now a Civil Rights Museum. It has the lunch counter where the Greensboro Four sat to protest unfair rules (History).

## Quiz

1. The Greensboro Four referred to _____.

    A) Four Black students.

    B) Four Black women.

    C) Four Black children.

2. The Greensboro Sit-In happened at which company?

    A) Target

    B) Walgreens

    C) Woolworths

3. Which organization was founded just two months after the Greensboro Sit-In?

    A) CNN

    B) SNCC

    C) NAACP

4. Which happened first?

    A) Freedom Rides

    B) March on Washington

    C) Greensboro Sit-In

## Activity

The Greensboro Four showed others how to stand up for fairness. They inspired people to do sit-ins in other towns. A sit-in is when people sit quietly in a place to show they want to change something unfair. They stay peaceful and don't hurt or fight anyone. The Greensboro Four also encouraged a group of students to help. They started a group called the Student Nonviolent Coordinating Committee (SNCC). It worked on ideas and planned peaceful protests like the Freedom Riders and the March on Washington. They wanted to make things fair for everyone.

What are you doing today? Can you write a poem about how being fair makes the world a better place?

**Answers**

1. A
2. C
3. B
4. C

# Chapter Seven: Selma to Montgomery: The Long Walk to Freedom

Peaceful protests like the Greensboro Sit-In and the March on Washington were very important. They showed that even though Black people had the right to vote, many could not. Southern states made it hard for them to vote. Even though they had rights on paper, the reality was different.

In 1868, the Fourteenth Amendment made Black people U.S. citizens. In 1870, the Fifteenth Amendment gave Black men the right to vote. But by 1964, voting was still very hard and dangerous for African Americans.

### African Americans and Voting

Voting means choosing leaders who can protect your rights. In the 1950s, it was very hard for Black people to vote. In many places, like the Southern states, Black people had to follow unfair rules to be able to vote. These rules stopped them from voting. Some people tried to help Black Americans register to vote. They held events to help them sign up. But helping was risky and dangerous. In the 1950s, Reverend Lee, a minister in Mississippi, was killed for helping Black people register (Library of Congress).

## Literacy Tests

*Literacy* means the ability to read and write. In some Southern states, Black people were not allowed to learn to read or write. They were not free and had to work under their White masters without pay. This was a problem. In 1900, 50 percent of Black men who could vote couldn't read. Among the White people, the percentage of illiterate people was 12 (Evans, Farrell). In the 1960s, people had to take reading tests to vote. Many White people who couldn't read didn't have to take the test. A rule called the grandfather clause protected them. It let them vote if their grandfathers had voted before the Civil War (Evans, Farrell). But Black people had to take the test.

### Poll Taxes

People had to pay money, called a poll tax, to vote. Black people earned less money than White people and didn't have as many job chances. Most couldn't afford to pay the tax. This meant many African Americans couldn't vote.

## Selma to Montgomery March

Selma to Montgomery March. '

The Civil Rights Act of 1964 became law on July 2, 1964. President Lyndon Johnson signed it. This law banned segregation in public places. It also stopped unfair voting rules like literacy tests and poll taxes (History). Even with the law, Black people still had trouble voting.

In 1965, Martin Luther King Jr. worked to help Black voters in Selma, Alabama. Only 2 out of 100 Black people there were able to register (History). This was because of unfair rules. Some leaders, like Governor George Wallace, worked hard to stop Black people from voting (History).

**Bloody Sunday**

On February 18, 1965, a peaceful protest happened in Marion, Alabama. White people attacked the protesters. An officer from the state police shot a young Black man named Jimmie Lee Jackson during the unrest. Jackson died (History).

After this, King and others planned a big march. They wanted to walk 54 miles from Selma to Montgomery, Alabama.

The march started on March 7, 1965. Protesters crossed a bridge in Selma. But state troopers attacked them. They used whips, nightsticks, and tear gas. The protesters were forced back. This became known as "Bloody Sunday." TV cameras recorded the attack. People all over the country saw the violence. Many were shocked. Hundreds of people came to Selma to join the protests.

Dr. King led another march to the Edmund Pettus Bridge on March 9. State troopers blocked them again, but this time, there was no violence. Finally, on March 21, the protesters started their long walk to Montgomery. President Johnson sent soldiers to protect them. The marchers made it safely to the capital (History).

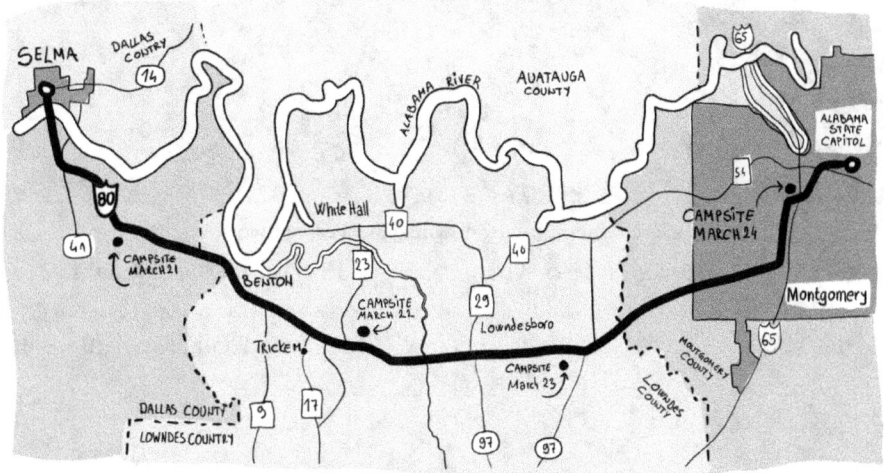

The group marched for 12 hours every day and slept in the fields at night. They were very brave. Even though they faced danger, they never gave up. After four days, on March 25, they reached Montgomery. There, nearly 50,000 Black and White supporters welcomed them.

President Johnson was impressed by their peaceful march. He found it was not just a problem for Black people. It was a problem for all Americans. Everyone must work together to overcome unfairness and hate. He said, "And we shall overcome" (History).

The march and the violence people saw on TV changed many minds. It led to the Voting Rights Act of 1965. This law stopped unfair rules that made it hard for Black people to vote. The courage of the marchers inspired many people to join the fight for fairness and equality. Their actions changed history forever.

President Lyndon Johnson signing the Voting Rights Act. [10]

While people walked to Montgomery, President Johnson talked to Congress. He asked for a law to help Black people vote (History). In August 1965, Congress made a new law. This law let Black people vote.

## Quiz

Let's see how much you remember! Can you put these events in the right order? Start with what happened first.

- Rosa Parks gets arrested for not giving up her bus seat to a White person.
- Ruby Bridges attends an all-White school.
- The Little Rock Nine children go to an all-White school.
- The burning of a Freedom Riders bus happened.
- Martin Luther King Jr. gives his "I Have a Dream" speech after the March on Washington.
- Selma to Montgomery March took place.

## Activity

Make a list of things you care about and would walk a long way to help fix. What's important to you? Is it helping the planet, better school lunches, homes for people without houses, or something else? Write down what you would like to change and why it matters to you!

**Answers:**

- Rosa Parks gets arrested for not giving up her bus seat to a White person.
- The Little Rock Nine children go to an all-White school.
- Ruby Bridges attends an all-White school.
- The burning of a Freedom Riders bus happened.
- Martin Luther King Jr. gave his "I Have a Dream Speech" after the March on Washington.
- Selma to Montgomery March took place.

# Chapter Eight: The Civil and Voting Rights Acts

Before the Civil Rights Act of 1964 and the Voting Rights Act of 1965, life was unfair for Black people. They couldn't go to some parks or movie theaters. On buses and trains, they had to sit in separate areas. Water fountains were labeled "colored" or "White." Black workers were paid less than White workers and had a hard time getting good jobs. Black children went to separate schools.

There were laws, like the Fourteenth and Fifteenth Amendments, that were supposed to give Black people the same rights as everyone else. These laws gave the right to vote. Many southern states didn't follow these laws. They made new rules, like reading tests and poll taxes, to stop Black people from voting. These unfair rules changed with The Civil Rights Act and Voting Rights Act.

### Civil Rights Act of 1964

The fight for fairness started long before 1964. In 1955, Rosa Parks was arrested for not giving up her bus seat to a White man. Her brave action led to the Montgomery Bus Boycott. This inspired many other protests over the next 10 years.

Martin Luther King Jr. joined Rosa's fight. He worked with other leaders, like John Lewis, to plan peaceful protests. They helped organize the March on Washington. At the march, Martin gave his famous "I Have a Dream" speech. His words still inspire people today.

Groups like the National Association for the Advancement of Colored People (NAACP) worked hard to help people fight for fairness. It helped pass important laws, like the Civil Rights Act of 1957 and 1964, the Voting Rights Act of 1965, and the Fair Housing Act of 1968.

In 1961, President John F. Kennedy didn't want to make new civil rights laws. But in the South, people were marching for their rights. In Birmingham, Alabama, police attacked peaceful marchers. They used dogs, clubs, and strong water hoses to hurt them (History). This made Kennedy change his mind.

In 1963, Kennedy asked for stronger laws to protect Black people. He said, "The United States will not be fully free until all of its people are free" (History). Later that year, Kennedy was killed. After he died, Lyndon B. Johnson became President. In his first big speech, Johnson said, "Let this Congress be the one that does more for civil rights than ever before" (History).

President Lyndon B. Johnson signing the Civil Rights Act. ¹¹

On July 2, 1964, President Lyndon B. Johnson signed the Civil Rights Act. He signed it using 75 pens. After signing, the President gave away the pens to special people, like Martin Luther King Jr. (History). It was now unlawful to treat people unfairly because of their skin color or religion.

Black people could now go to parks, restaurants, and other public places without being told they couldn't. The law also made it wrong for bosses to treat workers unfairly because of their race or gender. It stopped unfair voting rules, like making people take hard reading tests or pay extra taxes to vote.

Martin Luther King Jr. named the Civil Rights Act a "second emancipation." It set Black people free. Can you say what was the first emancipation? It was when President Abraham Lincoln freed the slaves in 1863. The Civil Rights Act helped create other important laws, like the Voting Rights Act in 1965 and the Fair Housing Act in 1968.

### The Voting Rights Act of 1965

Even after the Civil Rights Act, many Black people still couldn't vote. Unfair tests and taxes were still used to stop them. Some voting workers told Black voters they were in the wrong place. Others said their forms were filled out wrong. Some were even turned away for small mistakes, like putting the wrong date on their papers. President Johnson talked about these unfair rules. He said some Black voters had to read the whole Constitution or explain very hard laws (History).

The Selma to Montgomery march showed everyone how unfair things were. The whole country saw it and demanded change. This helped leaders pass the Voting Rights Act.

On August 6, 1965, President Johnson signed the Voting Rights Act; Martin Luther King Jr. and other civil rights leaders were there to watch. This law was even stronger than the Civil Rights Act of 1964. It stopped literacy tests and let the federal government take charge of voting areas. This made it easier for Black people to register to vote (History).

Even with the new law, things were still hard for Black people. Some local officers didn't follow the rules. But the law gave Black people a way to fight against unfair rules. Over time, more Black people were able to vote (History).

## Quiz

Can you tell what is true and what is not? Try to decide if these statements are fact (true) or fiction (false).

1. President John F. Kennedy signed the Civil Rights Act of 1964.
2. The Selma to Montgomery March happened after the Voting Rights Act was signed.
3. The Montgomery Bus Boycott is considered to be the event that started a decade of mass protests.
4. Martin Luther King Jr. was present at the signing of both the Civil Rights and Voting Rights Acts.
5. President Lyndon B. Johnson signed both acts.

## Activity

Can you list five important things you learned from this chapter?

**Answers**

1. Fiction
2. Fiction
3. Fact
4. Fact
5. Fact

# Chapter Nine: The Fair Housing Act and Equal Housing Rights

## The Fair Housing Act and Equal Housing Rights

Imagine not being able to live in a place just because of your skin color. Black families couldn't rent or buy homes in certain neighborhoods. Today, this seems unfair and hard to believe, but before the late 1960s, it was the reality for Black people. Even African Americans who fought in wars for the country, like World War II, had the same problem. They served their country but were still told they could only live in some parts of the city.

### Before the Housing Act

Two Supreme Court rules said it was unlawful to keep away Black families from certain areas. These were *Shelley v. Kraemer* in 1948 and *Jones v. Mayer Co.* in 1968. But even these rulings were not enough, and Black families still faced many problems. People were angry and unkind when they tried to move into some neighborhoods. Neighborhoods made rules to keep them out. Groups like the NAACP wanted new laws to let Black families live wherever they wanted (History).

The Fair Housing Act of 1968

Martin Luther King Jr. started marching in Chicago in 1966. He wanted everyone to see how unfair housing rules were for Black people. On April 4, 1968, the Senate planned to vote on a new housing law. This law was part of the Civil Rights Act of 1964.

Dr. King was in Memphis, Tennessee. He was helping workers who were on strike. While standing on the balcony of his hotel, Dr. King was shot and killed. He was only 39 years old.

After Dr. King died, President Johnson asked Congress to pass the Fair Housing Act quickly. He wanted it done before Dr. King's funeral to honor him. Congress passed the law on April 10, and President Johnson signed it on April 11 (History).

The Fair Housing Act was very important for civil rights. It was against the law to treat people unfairly when selling or renting homes. People could not be denied a home because of their skin color, religion, gender, or where they were from. This law finally gave African Americans the right to live wherever they wanted.

As time went on, the Fair Housing Act made neighborhoods friendlier places to live. People started to get used to the changes. This rule was a big step toward treating everyone the same.

Kids of color and White kids were already going to school together. From now on, they could live near each other. They could become friends and play together. People with kids could shop at the same places. They could go to the same places. It took over one hundred years for America to make rules that gave Black people the same rights as White people.

The fight for justice goes on even now. Even though the Fair Housing Act was a big step forward, we still need to do more. Everyone should be treated the same and feel like they belong.

## Quiz

If you could live anywhere, in any kind of house, what would it look like? Draw a picture of your perfect home.

# End-of-Book Quiz

1. The Greensboro Sit-In happened in what state?

    A) Mississippi

    B) Alabama

    C) North Carolina

2. How old was Ruby Bridges when she went to an all-White school?

    A) 12

    B) 6

    C) 8

3. T/F: The Freedom Riders were made up of all Black people.

4. T/F: Martin Luther King Jr. is still active in helping Blacks fight for equality.

5. Rosa Parks arrest started the _____.

    A) Freedom Rides through the South

    B) Civil Rights Act of 1964

    C) Montgomery Bus Boycott

6. Which President signed both the Civil and Voting Rights Acts?

    A) Ronald Reagan

    B) Lyndon B. Johnson

    C) John F. Kennedy

7. What was the name of the bridge where the Selma to Montgomery March demonstrators were stopped?

    A) Edmund Pettus Bridge

    B) Edward Petty Bridge

    C) Evan Prowers Bridge

8. The Little Rock Nine was _____.

    A) Where the Freedom Riders bus burned

    B) The name of the school where Ruby Bridges attended

    C) The nickname for the nine Black students who attended an all-White school.

9. T/F: The Civil Rights Act of 1964 forbade segregation because of race or religion in public places

10. Which law made it so Blacks could live in any neighborhoods they wanted?

    A) The Civil Rights Act

    B) The Fair Housing Act

    C) The Voting Rights Act

11. Bloody Sunday happened during which event?

    A) Montgomery Bus Boycott

    B) Greensboro Sit-In

    C) Selma to Montgomery March

12. Dr. King gave his "I Have a Dream" speech during _____.

    A) March on Washington

    B) Montgomery Bus Boycott

    C) Signing celebration of the Voting Rights Act

# Answers

1. C
2. B
3. F
4. F
5. C
6. B
7. A
8. C
9. T
10. B
11. C
12. A

# Check out another book in the series

# Welcome Aboard, Check Out This Limited-Time Free Bonus!

Ahoy, reader! Welcome to the Ahoy Publications family, and thanks for snagging a copy of this book! Since you've chosen to join us on this journey, we'd like to offer you something special.

Check out the link below for a FREE e-book filled with delightful facts about American History.

But that's not all - you'll also have access to our exclusive email list with even more free e-books and insider knowledge. Well, what are ye waiting for? Click the link below to join and set sail toward exciting adventures in American History.

Access your bonus here
https://ahoypublications.com/
Or, Scan the QR code!

# References

Biography. "Rosa Parks: Timeline of Her Life, Montgomery Bus Boycott and Death." Accessed on

November 6, 2024.https://www.biography.com/activists/rosa-parks-timeline-facts.

Bunch, Lonnie. "The Little Rock Nine." Smithsonian. National Museum of African American

History & Culture. Accessed on November 7, 2024. https://nmaahc.si.edu/explore/stories/little-rock-nine.

Encyclopedia of Alabama. "Segregation (Jim Crow)." Accessed on November 6, 2024.

https://encyclopediaofalabama.org/article/segregation-jim-crow/.

Evans, Farrell. "How Jim Crow-Era Laws Suppressed the African American Vote for

Generations." *History.* Accessed on November 26, 2024.

https://www.history.com/news/jim-crow-laws-Black-vote.

History. "Civil Rights Act of 1964." Accessed on November 27, 2024.

https://www.history.com/topics/Black-history/civil-rights-act.

History. "Fair Housing Act." Accessed on November 27, 2024.

https://www.history.com/topics/Black-history/fair-housing-act.

History. "Freedom Riders." Accessed on November 22, 2024.

https://www.history.com/topics/Black-history/freedom-rides.

History. "Greensboro Sit-In." Accessed on November 26, 2024.

https://www.history.com/topics/Black-history/the-greensboro-sit-in

History. "Selma to Montgomery March." Accessed November 26, 2024. https://www.history.com/topics/Black-history/selma-montgomery-march.

History. "Voting Rights Act of 1965." Accessed on November 27, 2024. https://www.history.com/topics/Black-history/voting-rights-act.

Jaynes. Gerald D. "Little Rock Nine. American Activists." Britannica. Accessed on November 7, 2024. https://www.britannica.com/topic/Little-Rock-Nine.

Library of Congress. "Voting Rights." Accessed on November 26, 2024. https://www.loc.gov/collections/civil-rights-history-project/articles-and-essays/voting-rights/.

Library of Congress. "African American Voting Rights." Accessed on November 26, 2024. https://www.loc.gov/classroom-materials/elections/voters/african-americans/.

National Museum of American History. "Freedom Struggle." Accessed on November 27, 2024. https://americanhistory.si.edu/brown/history/6-legacy/freedom-struggle-2.html.

National Park Service. "The Little Rock Nine." Accessed on November 7, 2024. https://www.nps.gov/people/the-little-rock-nine.htm.

Dawson, Shay. "Ruby Bridges." *National Women's History Museum.* Accessed on November 23, 2024. https://www.womenshistory.org/education-resources/biographies/ruby-bridges.

Gray, D. Ryan. "The Melpomene Neighborhood, 1930-1960." New Orleans Historical. Accessed on November 22, 2024. https://neworleanshistorical.org/items/show/1663.

Library of Congress. "Rosa Parks Arrested." Accessed on November 6, 2024. https://www.loc.gov/exhibitions/rosa-parks-in-her-own-words/about-this-exhibition/the-bus-boycott/rosa-parks-arrested/.

NAACP. "Rosa Parks." Accessed on November 6, 2024. https://naacp.org/find-resources/history-explained/civil-rights-leaders/rosa-parks.

National Archives. "The Student Nonviolent Coordinating Committee (SNCC)." *African American Heritage.* Accessed on November 22, 2024. https://www.archives.gov/research/african-americans/Black-power/sncc.

PBS. "Freedom to Travel." Accessed on November 24, 2024.

https://www.pbs.org/wgbh/americanexperience/features/freedom-riders-freedom-travel/#:~:text=Blacks%20were%20forced%20to%20sit,always%20present%20for%20Black%20travelers.

Stanford University. "Congress of Racial Equality (CORE)." *The Martin Luther King, Jr.*

*Research and Education Institute.* Accessed on November 22, 2024.
https://kinginstitute.stanford.edu/congress-racial-equality-core.

Stanford University. "March on Washington for Jobs and Freedom." *The Martin Luther King, Jr.*

*Research and Education Institution.* Accessed on November 22, 2024.
https://kinginstitute.stanford.edu/march-washington-jobs-and-freedom.

U.S. History. "54b. Rosa Parks and the Montgomery Bus Boycott." Pre-Columbian to the New

Millennium. Accessed on November 6, 2024.
https://www.ushistory.org/us/54b.asp?srsltid=AfmBOoqmRK86EllrWATRE27Hxb_bSXIOV_GQ8MBdjJ_tnC0mQAdtcIfK.

# Image Sources

1 https://commons.wikimedia.org/wiki/File:Elizabeth_Eckford.jpg

2 https://commons.wikimedia.org/wiki/File:Operation_Arkansas,_Little_Rock
_Nine.jpg

3 https://commons.wikimedia.org/wiki/File:March_on_Washington_for_Jobs
_and_Freedom,_Martin_Luther_King,_Jr._and_Joachim_Prinz_1963.jpg

4 David Erickson, CC BY 2.0 <https://creativecommons.org/licenses/by/2.0>, via
Wikimedia Commons:
https://commons.wikimedia.org/wiki/File:Martin_Luther_King_Jr._-
_I_Have_A_Dream_Speech.jpg

5 U.S. National Park Service, CC0, via Wikimedia Commons:
https://commons.wikimedia.org/wiki/File:Greyhound_Bus_Attack_Anniston_2.jpg

6 See file page for creator info:
https://commons.wikimedia.org/wiki/File:Negro_drinking_at_%22Colored%22_wat
er_cooler_in_streetcar_terminal,_Oklahoma_City,_Oklahoma_by_Russell_Lee.jpg

7 Uncredited DOJ photographer, restored by Adam Cuerden (a relatively minor
restoration), Public domain, via Wikimedia Commons:
https://commons.wikimedia.org/wiki/File:US_Marshals_with_Young_Ruby_Bridges
_on_School_Steps.jpg

8 https://commons.wikimedia.org/wiki/File:Civil_Rights_protesters_and_
Woolworth%27s_Sit-
In,_Durham,_NC,_10_February_1960._From_the_N%26O_Negative_Collection,
_State_Archives_of_North_Carolina,_Raleigh,_NC._Photos_taken_by_The_News
_%26_(24495308926).jpg

9 https://commons.wikimedia.org/wiki/File:Selma_to_Montgomery_Marches.jpg

10 https://commons.wikimedia.org/wiki/File:LyndonJohnson_signs_Voting_

Rights_Act_of_1965.jpg

11 https://commons.wikimedia.org/wiki/File:Lyndon_Johnson_signing_
Civil_Rights_Act,_July_2,_1964.jpg

www.ingramcontent.com/pod-product-compliance
Lightning Source LLC
Chambersburg PA
CBHW071542120626
46550CB00006B/2550